Brown Booby
Birds
of Cayman Brac

Text and Photographs by Bonnie Scott

 LYRIC POWER

ISBN: 9781674868172
BISAC Category *
Nonfiction > Nature > Animals > Birds
Nonfiction > Nature > Birdwatching Guides

For sales and Distribution Contact:
Elaine A. Powers at iginspired@gmail.com

Brown Booby Birds
of Cayman Brac

Text and Photographs by
Bonnie Scott

Perched on a piling on the wharf, soaring over the cliff edge on a current of air, plunge diving for fish, gliding home along the shore, the Brown Booby is a familiar sight in Cayman Brac. While this species is found on some Caribbean and Atlantic islands around the world, it is rarely found breeding on an inhabited island and, in the Cayman Islands, it is only found on Cayman Brac. The Brown Booby is not an endangered species worldwide but it is of concern in Cayman and is protected by law.

The Brown Booby is a handsome bird covered in rich brown feathers with a blazing white chest. That's why its scientific name is *Sula Leucogaster:* *Sula* for seabird, *leucogaster* for white stomach.

The juvenile form is grayish brown with darkening on the head, wings and tail and a blue-gray beak.

Brown Boobies are large birds, up to three feet long with a five-foot wingspan.

While Brown Boobies are usually silent, they can hiss or honk or quack when their nest is approached. People are requested by the Department of Environment to stay at least fifty feet away from boobies and their nests.

Nesting begins in late autumn. Birds nest on ledges on the bluff edge and on the ground near the sea. Nests can be built on vegetation, on rock, bare earth or sand, even on man-made structures.

Nest building is an important part of courtship and begins with the male finding desirable bits of branches or seaweed and offering these to the female. If she finds the gift and the male acceptable, the pair will begin arranging

twigs and other ground debris in a circular pattern. Twigs and interesting bits of dried seaweed make up most of the nest, although colorful pieces of rope and plastic are often added to the simple structure.

The female bird will begin sitting for hours every day and an egg should soon appear.

When the male begins sharing nest-
sitting duties, you will know that an egg
has been laid.

The sexes can be easily distinguished
by a slight color in the usual pale yellow
beak: pink for her, blue for him.

her

him

Sometimes a second egg will be laid but usually only one chick is raised. Parents take turns sitting continuously on the nest for about six weeks until the egg hatches and then another two weeks or so until the chick, which is hatched blind and helpless, can survive exposure.

For the first few weeks of the chick's life, one parent usually stays with it while the other flies off to feed at sea.   When the fishing parent returns, it feeds the chick by regurgitating some of its catch. Then it's the other parent's turn to leave the nest to fish.

Their food preference is ballyhoo, a baitfish that swims in large schools. They also eat flying fish and squid. Brown Boobies fish by plunging into the ocean or swooping to take fish on the surface.

After it is six weeks old, parents may both
be gone for short periods while the chick
stays alone on or near the nest.

Although the baby booby is featherless
when hatched, at about three weeks it is
covered with white down, almost as big
as the parents, and very, very cute.

Over the next three months the chick gradually gets its primary flight feathers, which appear dark against the white down.

This five-week-old booby chick is with its mother.

Fluffy seven-week-old chick is getting its flight feathers.

This eight-week-old chick has tail feathers!

Perched on the Bluff edge, the still-fluffy chick appears bigger than its father but is only nine weeks old.

As its fuzzy down falls out and more feathers grow, the chick loses some of that cuteness and instead will make you laugh. Here it is at about ten weeks.

More and more feathers appear until the juvenile bird is fully feathered in a blend of light browns and gray and it begins the clumsy attempt to fly.
Eleven to twelve weeks old.

All the down is gone and the fourteen-week-old juvenile is ready to fly.   It flies longer distances every day but doesn't stray too far from the nest because its parents are still feeding it. The sky over nesting sites is busy, filled with parents setting out or returning from fishing expeditions and juveniles practicing flight. Juveniles begin to imitate the adult birds in learning to snatch food from the sea but parents will continue to feed them until they are six or seven months old.

About half the year is spent near the nesting ground. When the juvenile is independent, Brown Boobies venture away, spending more time foraging at sea, riding air currents, and perching by the sea preening and waterproofing their feathers by applying oil secreted from a gland at the base of the tail.

The perching and preening Brown Boobies are a photogenic favorite of tourists. Good places to see them are at the very westernmost end of the island, past the Westerly Ponds, at Scott Dock, at Panama Canal, and on the Lighthouse path. During breeding season, some Brown Boobies nest on the Bluff edge, particularly near the Lighthouse, and some can be seen along the shore on the south side.

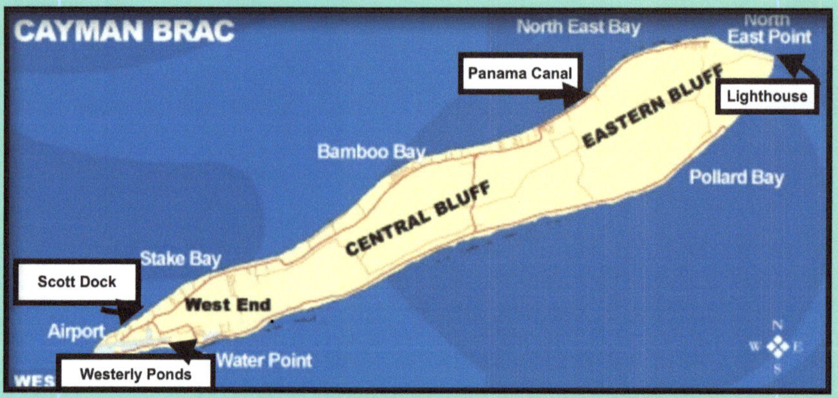

Because of human activities and introduced predators, Brown Boobies live mainly on remote islands away from these dangers, but the population on Cayman Brac does face the hazards of civilization.

At one time the booby was used as a food source but that is very uncommon now. Disturbance by beachgoers and hikers, particularly people approaching too closely, property development, and invasive species are problems. Domestic cats have taken a large toll on breeding Brown Boobies, particularly those nesting on lower ground.

Entanglement in fishing line can cause injury and death.

Another threat is pollution, particularly plastics in the water and on the shore. Major efforts are being made both by international and local environmental organizations and by individuals on Cayman Brac to reduce this harm.

You can help by buying fewer plastics, choosing more sustainable products, safely disposing of garbage, and recycling all materials possible in your area. Consider contributing to environmental organizations and supporting government policies that help to reduce plastic and clean the seas.

About The Author:

Bonnie Scott was trained in sea turtle conservation in Florida and brought that knowledge to Cayman Brac where she began the first turtle patrol on the island. She is a member of the species management team for the preservation of the Sister Isles Rock Iguana and is involved in rehabilitation of injured iguanas, turtles and birds. Bonnie was chosen as Environmentalist of the Year for the Cayman Islands. She resides on Cayman Brac.

Other Books by Bonnie:
Silent Rocks: Iguanas of Cayman Brac
by Elaine A Powers (Author), Anderson Atlas (Illustrator), Bonnie Scott Edwards (Photographer)

LYRIC POWER

www.ingramcontent.com/pod-product-compliance
Lightning Source LLC
Chambersburg PA
CBHW040244240726
48664CB00001B/261